ISAAC ASIMOV'S NEW LIBRARY OF THE UNIVERSE

NEAREST THE SUN:
THE PLANET MERCURY

BY ISAAC ASIMOV
WITH REVISIONS AND UPDATING BY FRANCIS REDDY

Gareth Stevens Publishing
MILWAUKEE

**For a free color catalog describing Gareth Stevens' list of high-quality books,
call 1-800-542-2595 (USA) or 1-800-461-9120 (Canada).
Gareth Stevens' Fax: (414) 225-0377.**

The reproduction rights to all photographs and illustrations in this book are controlled by the
individuals or institutions credited on page 32 and may not be reproduced without their permission.

Library of Congress Cataloging-in-Publication Data

Asimov, Isaac.
　　Nearest the Sun: the planet Mercury / by Isaac Asimov; with revisions
　and updating by Francis Reddy.
　　　　p. cm. — (Isaac Asimov's New library of the universe)
　　Rev. ed. of: Mercury: the quick planet. 1989.
　　Includes index.
　　ISBN 0-8368-1221-2
　　1. Mercury (Planet)—Juvenile literature. [1. Mercury (Planet).]
　I. Reddy, Francis, 1959. II. Asimov, Isaac. Mercury: the quick planet.
　III. Title. IV. Series: Asimov, Isaac. New library of the universe.
　QB611.A76　 1995
　523.4'1--dc20　　　　　　　　　　　　 95-7878

This edition first published in 1995 by
Gareth Stevens Publishing
1555 North RiverCenter Drive, Suite 201
Milwaukee, Wisconsin 53212, USA

Series editor: Barbara J. Behm
Design adaptation: Helene Feider
Production director: Teresa Mahsem
Editorial assistant: Diane Laska
Picture research: Matthew Groshek and Diane Laska

Printed in the United States of America

1 2 3 4 5 6 7 8 9 9 99 98 97 96 95

To bring this classic of young people's information up to date, the editors at Gareth
Stevens Publishing have selected two noted science authors, Greg Walz-Chojnacki
and Francis Reddy. Walz-Chojnacki and Reddy coauthored the recent book *Celestial
Delights: The Best Astronomical Events Through 2001*.

Walz-Chojnacki is also the author of the book *Comet: The Story Behind Halley's
Comet* and various articles about the space program. He was an editor of *Odyssey*,
an astronomy and space technology magazine for young people, for eleven years.

Reddy is the author of nine books, including *Halley's Comet*, *Children's Atlas of the
Universe*, *Children's Atlas of Earth Through Time*, and *Children's Atlas of Native
Americans*, plus numerous articles. He was an editor of *Astronomy* magazine for
several years.

CONTENTS

We live in an enormously large place – the Universe. It's just in the last fifty-five years or so that we've found out how large it probably is. It's only natural that we would want to understand the place in which we live, so scientists have developed instruments – such as radio telescopes, satellites, probes, and many more – that have told us far more about the Universe than could possibly be imagined.

We have seen planets up close. We have learned about quasars and pulsars, black holes, and supernovas. We have gathered amazing data about how the Universe may have come into being and how it may end. Nothing could be more astonishing.

One of the planets we have seen up close is Mercury, the planet nearest the Sun. Mercury is so close to the Sun that it is usually overwhelmed by the Sun's light when we try to observe it. That is one reason why, until recently, scientists knew very little about Mercury. That is changed now. Thanks to the invention of probes, scientists have gathered many amazing details about this small, "quick" planet.

Isaac Asimov

Small, yet Mighty

Mercury is a small planet. At 3,030 miles (4,875 kilometers) in diameter, it is only three-eighths the width of Earth. Mercury is the closest planet to the Sun – only 36 million miles (57.9 million km) away on the average; and it comes as close as 29 million miles (46.6 million km) as it orbits the Sun. This is almost 70 percent closer to the Sun than Earth.

The surface of any planet this close to the Sun is bound to get very hot – as hot as 660° Fahrenheit (348° Centigrade). This is hot enough to melt lead.

And since Mercury is so close to the Sun, the Sun's gravity pulls hard. Earth orbits the Sun at 18.6 miles (29.9 km) a second, but Mercury orbits at an average of 29.8 miles (47.9 km) a second. It is the "quick" planet.

Left: The planet Mercury as seen by the *Mariner 10* spacecraft in 1974. Mercury's rough, cratered surface resembles the Moon's.

Opposite: Glowing streams of molten metal pour into molds at a foundry. The surface of Mercury gets hot enough to melt lead.

A Day That is Longer Than A Year?

From our point of view on Earth, Mercury has an unusual relationship with the Sun. First of all, its closeness to the Sun gives it a small orbit. It moves so quickly that its trip around the Sun – its year – takes only 88 days. But Mercury turns very slowly on its axis, so the time from sunrise to sunrise – one Mercury day – is 176 Earth days. So Mercury's "day" is twice as long as its year!

Mercury turns on its axis with a steady speed, but its orbit is lopsided. When it is nearer the Sun, it moves faster. For that reason, the Sun appears uneven in Mercury's sky. From certain places on Mercury, you might see the Sun rise, then set (as though it had changed its mind), and then rise again! The same holds true for sunset, too – first the Sun would set, then rise briefly, and then set again.

? *Mercury – why the wacky orbit?*

Mercury's orbit is more elliptical, or lopsided, than any planetary orbit except Pluto's. Mercury's orbit is also more tipped against the general plane of planetary orbits than any orbit except Pluto's. Since Mercury is so near the Sun, wouldn't its orbit be nearly circular and in the plane of the Sun's equator, like the orbit of Venus? Why isn't this so in Mercury's case? Scientists do not know.

Right: In this illustration, the bright yellow area of Mercury's tipped, lopsided orbit lies above Earth's orbital plane *(shown in blue)*. The pink area lies below Earth's orbital plane. A red line shows the 7° tilt between the two orbital planes.

Opposite: Space suits on Mercury would have to withstand extreme heat and cold on a planet bathed in bright sunlight and deep shadows.

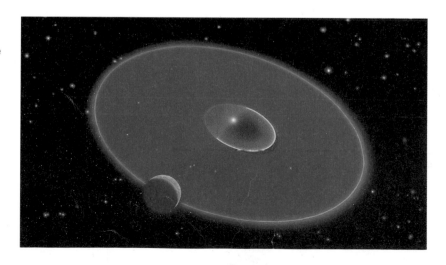

Metallic Mercury

When our Solar System came into being, the material outside the Sun turned into numerous small bodies. These small bodies gradually crashed into each other and formed larger bodies. The gravitational pull of the larger bodies attracted most of the remaining small bodies, and the planets formed.

Very close to the Sun, the lighter material boiled away. Mercury formed only out of rocks and metal – materials that have a very high melting point.

Like Venus and Earth, Mercury has a large metallic center. But of all the known planets in our Solar System, Mercury's metallic center seems to be the largest for its overall size.

❓*Magnetic Mercury?*

Earth and at least three of the four giant planets have magnetic fields. To have a magnetic field, a planet must have a liquid center that conducts electricity, and it must rotate swiftly so that it sets the liquid swirling. The Moon and Mars do not have liquid centers, so they have no magnetic fields. Mercury does not have a liquid center and it rotates very slowly, so it shouldn't have a magnetic field. But it does. It has a weak magnetic field, and astronomers do not understand why it does.

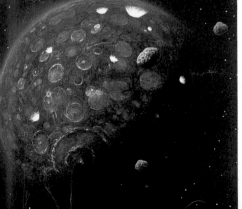

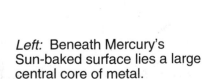

Left: Beneath Mercury's Sun-baked surface lies a large central core of metal.

Inset: Mercury's building blocks were rock and metal fragments.

Cratered Mercury

When a world forms, the last few bits of matter that strike it leave huge craters. If the particular world is like Earth, its water and atmosphere wear down these craters and make most of them disappear. If the world has volcanic action, lava from the volcanoes covers the surface and, again, most craters disappear.

Small worlds like Mercury usually don't have atmospheres or volcanic activity, so the marks left by the final collisions remain. There are many visible craters on Earth's Moon, for example. Mercury, meanwhile, is so hot that its surface remained soft for a long time. It is even more thickly covered with craters than the Moon!

Below: Both Earth's Moon *(left)* and Mercury *(right)* share the scars of collisions. A site on the Moon called the Mare Orientale looks very much like a similar basin on Mercury.

Right: Craters and bright "rays" of debris crowd Mercury's south polar area.

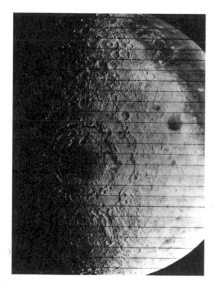

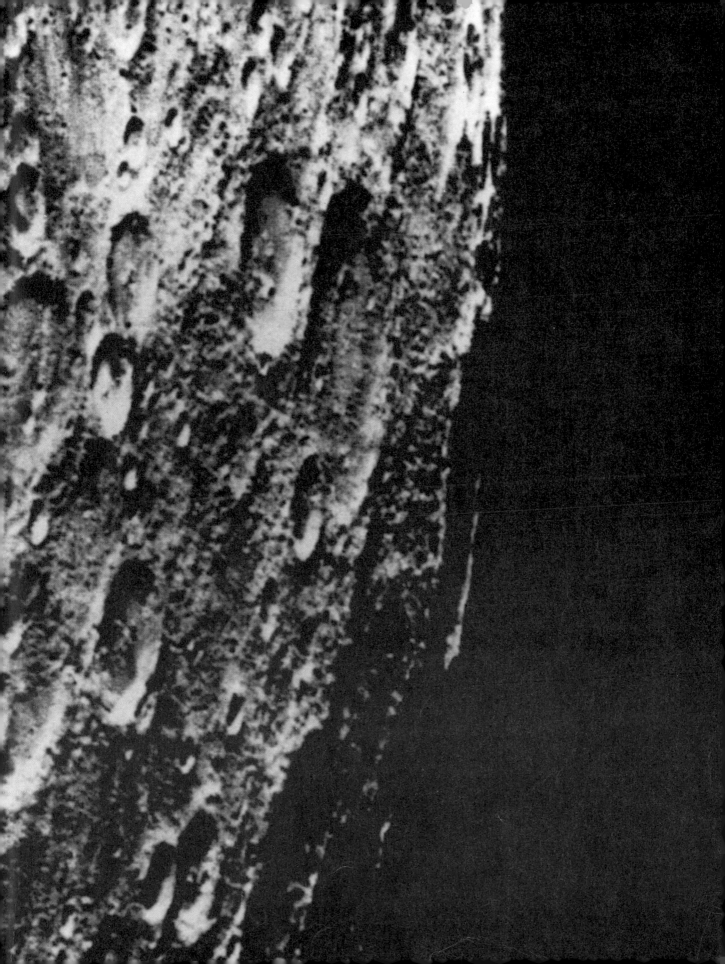

Crater Caloris

If Mercury could be viewed from Earth as closely as our Moon can be viewed, it would look very much like the Moon. It is thickly covered with craters that look somewhat smaller than those on the Moon. But that is only because Mercury is a larger body, so its craters look smaller by comparison.

Mercury's largest crater has the name *Caloris*, meaning "heat," because it has the highest temperatures on Mercury. Caloris is about 810 miles (1,300 km) across. There are also cliffs and fissures that pass right across the craters. This may be because Mercury shrank as it slowly cooled, and the surface of the planet cracked.

Left: The object that made the 810-mile- (1,300 km)- wide impact basin known as Caloris also formed a series of circular ridges on Mercury.

Below: An artist imagines the Caloris impact.

Mariner Visits Mercury

Mercury has long been a mystery to Earthbound skywatchers. In fact, until 1974, scientists didn't know anything about Mercury's surface. All that could be seen through a telescope was a small body near the Sun with vague shadows on it. The planet went through phases, like the Moon and Venus.

It was in 1974-1975 that a U.S. space probe, *Mariner 10*, changed our understanding of Mercury. *Mariner* passed within 168 miles (271 km) of Mercury's surface. Then, as it went around the Sun, *Mariner* visited Mercury twice more, coming as close as 203 miles (327 km) to the planet. It sent back to Earth detailed pictures of almost half of Mercury's surface.

Everything scientists know about the surface of Mercury comes from those pictures. No other craft has been sent to Mercury since.

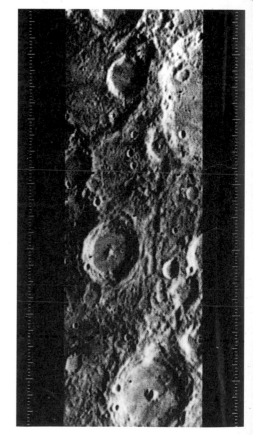

Right: Two views of Mercury – A rugged, cratered landscape *(top)*. The cracked floor of the Caloris basin *(bottom)*.

Opposite: The *Mariner 10* spacecraft. To survive so close to the Sun, it carried an umbrella-like sunshade *(shown in white)*.

Opposite, inset: Mariner 10 scanned Mercury's surface three times in 1974 and 1975, returning the pictures to Earth via radio beams.

Mercury's closeness to the Sun doesn't hinder observations from radio telescopes, such as the Very Large Array (VLA) in New Mexico *(bottom right)* and the Arecibo telescope in Puerto Rico *(opposite)*.

Opposite, inset: The VLA radio telescope measured Mercury's temperature to create this map, shaded so that hotter areas are brighter. Mercury's "hot poles" can easily be seen.

Below: By comparing radar maps with *Mariner 10* photographs of Mercury's polar regions, scientists find that the floors of many craters seem to reflect radar as well as ice! Will future astronauts one day ski on Mercury?

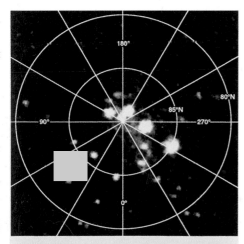

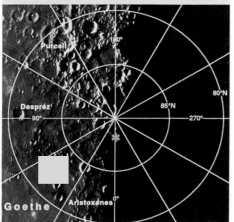

Ice on a Sun-baked World?

Mercury is certainly a Sun-baked planet, but some places on the planet are much hotter than others. Mercury's lopsided orbit, together with the relationship between its year and day, cause two areas along its equator to heat up much more than other parts of the planet. Astronomers refer to these locations as "hot poles." Whenever Mercury is closest to the Sun, one of these spots heats up to 800° F (427° C)!

Even stranger, scientists believe they have found ice on Mercury! In the 1990s, they beamed radar from radio telescopes on Earth to Mercury. The waves bounced off the planet's north and south polar regions and returned. Many large craters reflected the radar as well as icy moons of the outer Solar System. Near Mercury's north and south poles, sunlight never shines into the floors of some craters – so it's possible that ice may be buried on Mercury!

Earth to Mercury

In earlier times, before spacecraft, astronomers could only see Mercury from Earth as a bright, starlike object. Of the five planets (not counting Earth) that can be seen without a telescope, Mercury was probably the last to be discovered. Even with a telescope, it looks small.

When Mercury is nearest Earth, the Sun is on the other side of it. During these times, Earth faces Mercury's nighttime surface. This means Mercury can only be seen from Earth as a tiny, dark disk as it crosses in front of the surface of the Sun.

When Mercury is on the other side of the Sun, its day side *could* be seen from Earth, except for one problem – the Sun hides it. Mercury can only be seen well from Earth when it is located to one side of the Sun. Then it is seen only as a tiny speck.

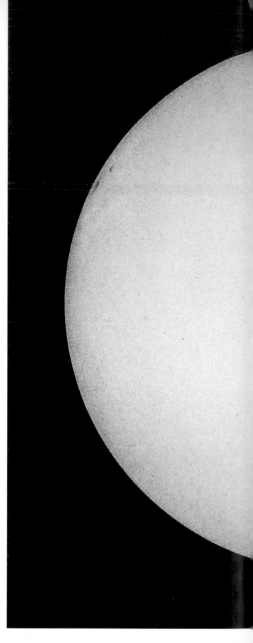

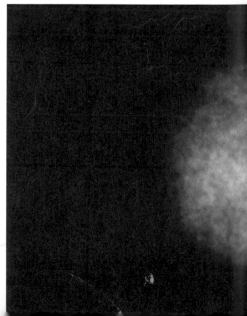

Opposite, top right: Mercury passes between Earth and the Sun. These drawings are based on observations made in 1960.

Top, left: The full disk of the Sun. Mercury is the tiny black dot near *bottom center.*

Bottom: The best views of Mercury from telescopes on Earth don't tell scientists much about the little planet. Even after the Sun sets, Mercury can only be seen through the thickest part of Earth's atmosphere, which blurs the image.

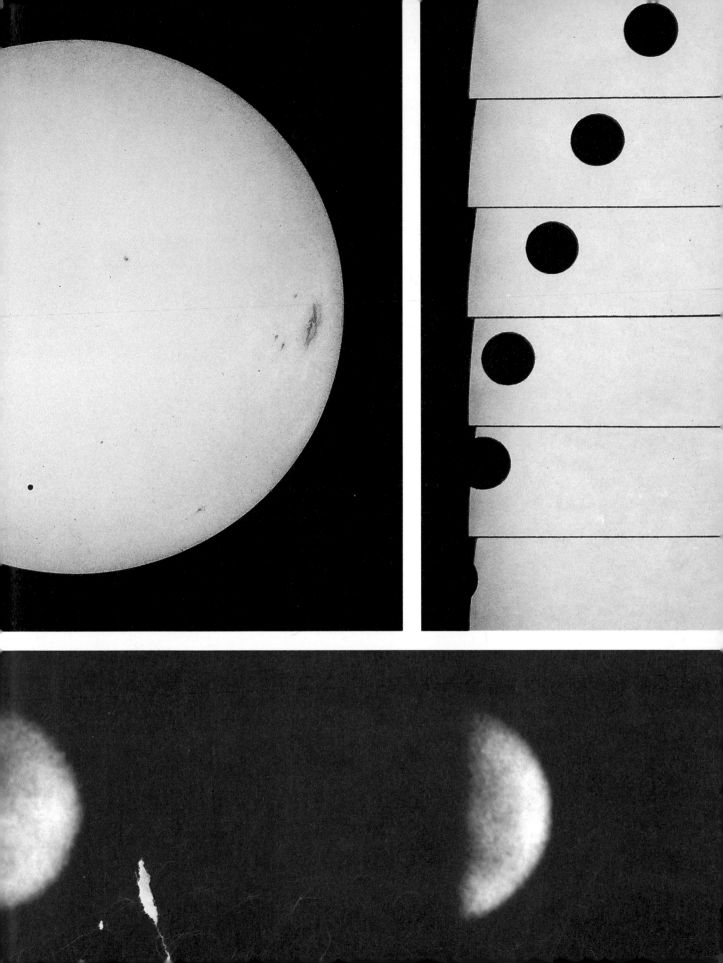

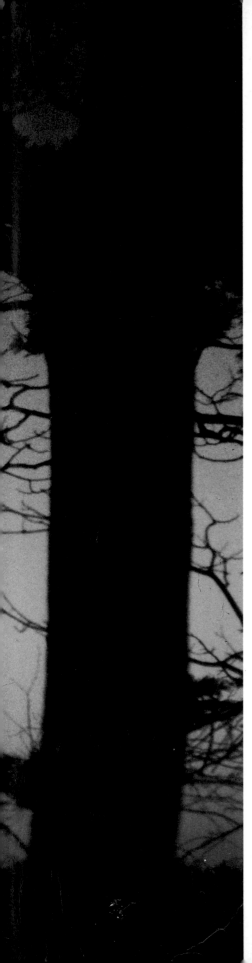

At Twilight and Dawn

Because Mercury is closer to the Sun than Earth is, we always see it quite close to the Sun. Look for it in the eastern sky just before sunrise, or in the western sky just after sunset.

In the evening, Mercury is visible for just under an hour or so after the Sun sets. And at dawn, Mercury is in the sky up to just under an hour before the Sun rises. Of course, by the time the Sun rises, our view of Mercury is over.

To find Mercury, search for it in the twilight or the dawn.

! Looking for Mercury – to see or not to see

Even around sunset or sunrise, Mercury is often so close to the Sun that it is hard to see. The sky is so bright just after sunset or just before sunrise that little Mercury can be missed. In 1543, Polish astronomer Nicolaus Copernicus explained that the planets circle the Sun; they don't circle Earth. Even Earth itself circles the Sun. Copernicus was one of the most famous astronomers ever, yet not once did even he manage to catch sight of Mercury.

Far left: Mercury and the crescent Moon. The entire disk of the Moon is dimly visible, illuminated by sunlight reflected from Earth.

Left: Polish astronomer Nicolaus Copernicus, the man who argued that the planets circled the Sun.

The Messenger Mercury

Most of the planets are named after ancient gods. Mercury, the messenger of the ancient Roman gods, is usually pictured with wings on his feet. These represent how rapidly he moved when he was carrying his messages. Because the planet Mercury moves across the sky more rapidly than the other planets, it was named for this speedy messenger of the gods.

Metals were sometimes named for the planets, too. A certain metal looks like silver but is liquid. It was given the name *quicksilver*, which means "live silver." *Quicksilver* was also named for its "quickness" – so it was also referred to as *mercury*. Mercury is the silver liquid in a thermometer.

Below, left: This 1942 U.S. dime is called a Mercury dime. It shows the goddess of liberty wearing a winged helmet.

Below, right: The metal mercury, or quicksilver, forms shiny liquid drops at room temperature.

Opposite: Mercury, messenger of the gods.

! *Quick Mercury – fast and fooling the ancients*

The ancients believed that the faster an object moves across the sky, the nearer to Earth it must be. The Moon moves faster than any other object, so it had to be closest to Earth. They were right about that. But Mercury moves faster than Venus, so they thought Mercury was closer to Earth than Venus. Today, we know that Mercury moves as fast as it does because it is near the Sun, not Earth. Venus is closer to Earth than Mercury is.

The Odd Motion of Mercury

Mercury moves in its orbit because it is held by the Sun's gravity. The other planets also pull on it slightly. But when all these gravitational pulls were calculated, it turned out that there was a tiny motion of Mercury that couldn't be explained.

Could this motion be caused by the pull of an undiscovered planet even closer to the Sun? For a time, it was thought there might be such a planet called Vulcan, named after the god of fire. In more than fifty years of observation, however, astronomers never found this planet. Then scientist Albert Einstein discovered a new theory of gravity that accounted for Mercury's odd motion.

?Mercury's neighbors – getting an inside track on the Sun?

Some objects approach the Sun more closely than Mercury does. The asteroid Icarus comes within about 17 million miles (28 million km) of the Sun, and some comets come even closer. If instruments could be placed near Mercury's poles, where the Sun is always near the horizon and it may not be too hot, scientists could study these close approaches. They might even be able to study the Sun itself and get close-up answers to its many mysteries.

Top: Albert Einstein, the physicist who explained Mercury's odd movements.

Center: When a total solar eclipse occurred, it gave astronomers a perfect chance to see if there was an undiscovered planet closer to the Sun than Mercury.

Left: It was once thought that an unknown planet caused the odd motion of Mercury. The undiscovered planet was even given the name *Vulcan*, named after the ancient god of fire.

Uncovering Mercury's Mysteries

Mariner 10 has mapped less than half of Mercury's surface. There may be many more interesting discoveries to be made on the rest of the Sun's nearest planetary neighbor.

Scientists would like to study the interior of Mercury. Does Mercury experience earthquakes? It is possible that there are ice deposits deep within Mercury's polar craters. Studying the layers of ice will reveal much about Mercury's past. Ice will also help make it possible for humans to live and work on Mercury. The ice would supply water and oxygen for humans to survive, plus hydrogen that could be used as fuel.

But Mercury may not be a planet that humans would ever live on. It is too close to the Sun. It would be fascinating, however, to explore more of the inner reaches of our Solar System, as well as its outer reaches.

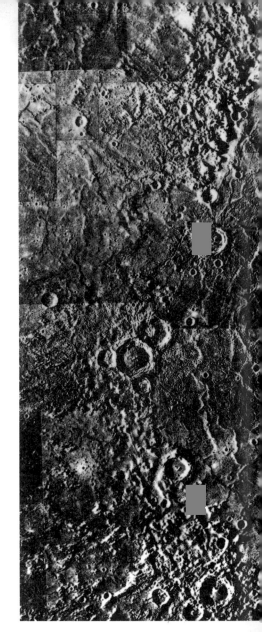

❗ *Tiny Mercury – small, but not a lightweight*

We used to think Mercury was the smallest planet. Now we know Pluto is even smaller. Even so, Mercury is smaller than some moons. Jupiter's largest moon, Ganymede, and Saturn's largest moon, Titan, are both larger than Mercury.

But those moons seem to be made of mainly icy material, while Mercury is made of rock and metal. If you could put worlds on a scale, Mercury would weigh more than twice as much as either of those large, icy satellites.

Opposite, top: The fractured Caloris basin on Mercury.

Above: As Mercury's interior cooled and shrank, its surface crust buckled and cracked – just as this apple's skin wrinkled as the apple dried out and shrank.

Left: Sunrise on Mercury.

27

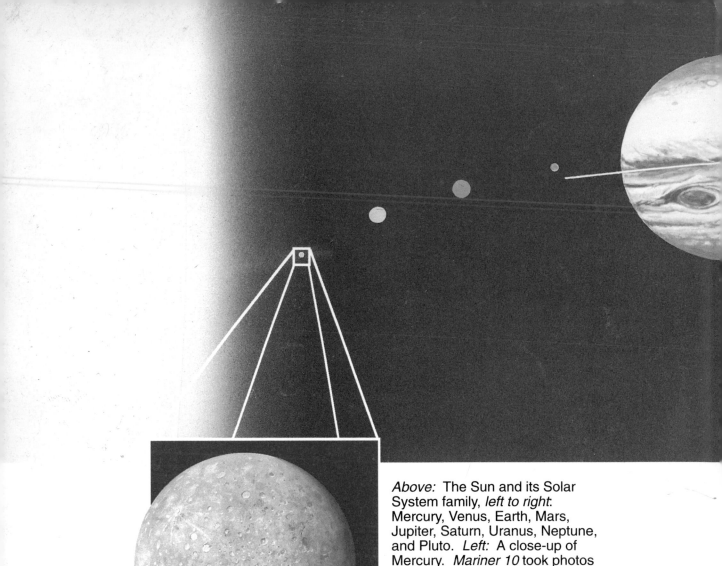

Above: The Sun and its Solar System family, *left to right:* Mercury, Venus, Earth, Mars, Jupiter, Saturn, Uranus, Neptune, and Pluto. *Left:* A close-up of Mercury. *Mariner 10* took photos that show Mercury's surface is even more heavily cratered than our Moon's.

Mercury: How It Measures Up to Earth

Planet	Diameter	Rotation Period	Period of Orbit around Sun (length of year)	Moons	Surface Gravity	Distance from Sun (nearest-farthest)	Least Time It Takes Light to Travel to Earth
Mercury	3,030 miles (4,875 km)	58.6 days*	88.0 days	0	0.38**	28.5-43.3 million miles (45.9-69.7 million km)	4.4 minutes
Earth	7,925 miles (12,753 km)	23 hours, 56 minutes	365.25 days (one year)	1	1.00**	91-94 million miles (147-152 million km)	—

* Mercury rotates, or spins on its axis, once every 58.6 days. It rotates 3 times for every 2 trips it makes around the Sun. Because Mercury rotates so slowly, the Sun stays up in Mercury's sky far longer than in Earth's sky. So from Mercury's surface, a solar "day" (sunrise to sunrise) lasts 176 days.

** Multiply your weight by this number to find out how much you would weigh on this planet.

Fact File: The "Quick" Planet

Mercury, the closest planet to the Sun, is the second smallest known planet in our Solar System. Only Pluto is smaller. Because Mercury doesn't have an atmosphere, it has no real "weather" as we know it on Earth – only incredibly hot days, and nights just as incredibly cold. Like Venus, Mercury has no moons.

Because Mercury is so hard to see from Earth, not much was known about it until the 1960s and 1970s. Since the planet only appeared as a tiny speck that went through phases like the Moon, scientists did not know what Mercury's surface was like. But thanks to *Mariner 10* and other efforts to learn more about this planet, we now understand many things about Mercury that were once mysteries. But there's still a lot to learn about the "quick" planet.

Even if human beings could visit Mercury one day in the future, not many would want to live there. By studying Mercury, however, we can learn about the history of our Solar System – including our own Earth.

More Books about Mercury

Journey to the Planets. Lauber (Crown)
Our Planetary System. Asimov (Gareth Stevens)
The Planets. Couper (Franklin Watts)
The Solar System. Lambert (Franklin Watts)
Wonders Around the Sun. Bonner (Lantern)

Videos

Astronomy 101: A Beginner's Guide to the Night Sky. (Mazon)
Mercury: The Quick Planet. (Gareth Stevens)
There Goes A Starship. (KidVision)

Places to Visit

You can explore Mercury and other parts of the Universe without leaving Earth.
Here are some museums and centers where you can find a variety of space exhibits.

NASA Lewis Research Center
Educational Services Office
21000 Brookpark Road
Cleveland, OH 44135

Henry Crown Science Center
Museum of Science and Industry
57th Street and Lake Shore Drive
Chicago, IL 60637

NASA Goddard Space Flight Center
Greenbelt Road
Greenbelt, MD 20771

Edmonton Space and Science Centre
11211 - 142nd Street
Edmonton, Alberta K5M 4A1

Perth Observatory
Walnut Road
Bickley, W.A. 6076 Australia

Ontario Science Centre
770 Don Mills Road
Don Mills, Ontario M3C 1T3

Places to Write

Here are some places you can write for more information about Mercury. Be sure to state what
kind of information you would like. Include your full name and address so they can write back
to you.

Jet Propulsion Laboratory
Public Affairs 180-201
4800 Oak Grove Drive
Pasadena, CA 91109

Canadian Space Agency
Communications Department
6767 Route de L'Aeroport
Saint Hubert, Quebec J3Y 8Y9

Sydney Observatory
P. O. Box K346
Haymarket 2000 Australia

National Space Society
922 Pennsylvania Avenue SE
Washington, D.C. 20003

Glossary

asteroids: very small "planets" made of rock or metal. There are thousands of them in our Solar System, and they mainly orbit the Sun between Mars and Jupiter. Some show up elsewhere in the Solar System – some as meteoroids and some possibly as "captured" moons of planets, such as Mars.

astronomer: a person involved in the scientific study of the Universe and its various bodies.

atmosphere: the gases that surround a planet, star, or moon.

axis: the imaginary straight line around which a planet, star, or moon turns, or spins.

black hole: a massive object – usually a collapsed star – so tightly packed that not even light can escape the force of its gravity.

Copernicus, Nicolaus: a Polish astronomer who was the first to argue that the Sun, not Earth, was the center of our Solar System and that the planets revolved around the Sun.

crater: a hole or pit caused by a volcanic explosion or the impact of a meteorite.

Einstein, Albert: a German-born U.S. scientist. His many theories include those concerning unusual motions in Mercury's orbit. He is perhaps the best-known scientist of the twentieth century.

elliptical: shaped like an oval. Mercury's orbit around the Sun is more elliptical than that of any other planet except Pluto.

fissure: a long, narrow crack, as in a rock or cliff face.

Icarus: an asteroid that approaches the Sun even more closely than Mercury does. It was named after a mythological boy whose father made him wings of wax and feathers. He flew too close to the Sun and his wings melted, so he tumbled to the sea below.

magnetic field: a field or area around a planet, such as Earth, with a center of melted iron. The magnetic field is caused by the planet's rotation, which makes the melted iron in the planet's core swirl. As a result, the planet is like a huge magnet.

orbit: the path that one celestial object follows as it circles, or revolves around, another.

phases: the periods when an object in space is partly or fully lit by the Sun. Like Earth's Moon, Mercury passes through phases as we watch it from Earth.

pole: either end of the axis around which a planet, moon, or star rotates.

probe: a craft that travels in space, photographing celestial bodies and even landing on some of them.

pulsar: a star with all the mass of an ordinary large star but with its mass squeezed into a small ball. It sends out rapid pulses of light or electrical waves.

rotate: to turn or spin on an axis.

satellite: a smaller body orbiting a larger body. The Moon is Earth's natural satellite. *Sputnik 1* and *2* were Earth's first artificial satellites.

Index

Born in 1920, Isaac Asimov came to the United States as a young boy from his native Russia. As a young man, he was a student of biochemistry. In time, he became one of the most productive writers the world has ever known. His books cover a spectrum of topics, including science, history, language theory, fantasy, and science fiction. His brilliant imagination gained him the respect and admiration of adults and children alike. Sadly, Isaac Asimov died shortly after the publication of the first edition of *Isaac Asimov's Library of the Universe.*

The publishers wish to thank the following for permission to reproduce copyright material: front cover, © Rick Sternbach; 4, © Stan Christensen, Courtesy of Beloit Corporation; 4-5, NASA; 6, © Julian Baum 1988; 7, © Pat Rawlings 1988; 8-9 (large), © Lynette Cook 1988; 8-9 (inset), © Dorothy Sigler Norton; 10 (left), NASA; 10 (right), © Larry Ortiz; 10-11, Jet Propulsion Laboratory; 12-13, NASA; 13, © Rick Sternbach; 14 (both), NASA; 15 (large), Jet Propulsion Laboratory; 15 (inset), NASA; 16 (large), Courtesy of NAIC; 16 (inset), Courtesy of Michael J. Ledlow; 17 (left, both), Courtesy of *Sky & Telescope* Magazine; 17 (right), Courtesy of NRAO/AUI; 18-19 (upper), © Richard Baum 1988; 18-19 (lower), Courtesy of New Mexico State University Observatory; 19, © Richard Baum 1988; 20-21, © Dennis Milon; 21, AIP Niels Bohr Library; 22 (left), Collection of Moshe ben-Shimon; 22 (right), Matthew Groshek/© Gareth Stevens, Inc.; 23, 24-25, © Keith Ward 1988; 25 (upper), AIP Niels Bohr Library; 25 (lower), 26, NASA; 26-27, © David A. Hardy; 27, The University of Chicago Library; 28, © Sally Bensusen 1988; 28-29, © Sally Bensusen 1987.